Man Plans

The Essential Daily Planner for Men

Daybook Heaven Books

DAYBOOK HEAVEN

B O O K S

Copyright 2016

Essential Daily Planner for Men

DATE

☐ ☐ ☐ ☐ ☐ ☐ ☐
Mon Tues Wed Thu Fri Sat Sun

Appointment	**Office**

General plan	**House**

Reminder	

Time	Activity Description	**Hobbies**
12:00 am		
1:00		
2:00		
3:00		
4:00		
5:00		
6:00		
7:00		
8:00		
9:00		
10:00		
11:00		
12:00pm		
1:00		
2:00		
3:00		
4:00		
5:00		
6:00		
7:00		
8:00		
9:00		
10:00		

Essential Daily Planner for Men

DATE

☐ ☐ ☐ ☐ ☐ ☐ ☐
Mon Tues Wed Thu Fri Sat Sun

	Appointment		**Office**

	General plan		**House**

	Reminder		

Time	Activity Description	**Hobbies**
12:00 am		
1:00		
2:00		
3:00		
4:00		
5:00		
6:00		
7:00		
8:00		
9:00		
10:00		
11:00		
12:00pm		
1:00		
2:00		
3:00		
4:00		
5:00		
6:00		
7:00		
8:00		
9:00		
10:00		

Essential Daily Planner for Men

DATE

☐ ☐ ☐ ☐ ☐ ☐ ☐
Mon Tues Wed Thu Fri Sat Sun

Appointment	**Office**

General plan	**House**

Reminder	

Time	Activity Description	**Hobbies**
12:00 am		
1:00		
2:00		
3:00		
4:00		
5:00		
6:00		
7:00		
8:00		
9:00		
10:00		
11:00		
12:00pm		
1:00		
2:00		
3:00		
4:00		
5:00		
6:00		
7:00		
8:00		
9:00		
10:00		

Essential Daily Planner for Men

DATE

☐ ☐ ☐ ☐ ☐ ☐ ☐
Mon Tues Wed Thu Fri Sat Sun

Appointment	**Office**
_____	_____
_____	_____
_____	_____
_____	_____

General plan	**House**
_____	_____
_____	_____
_____	_____
_____	_____

Reminder	
_____	_____
_____	_____
_____	_____

Time	Activity Description	**Hobbies**
12:00 am		_____
1:00		_____
2:00		_____
3:00		_____
4:00		_____
5:00		_____
6:00		_____
7:00		_____
8:00		_____
9:00		_____
10:00		_____
11:00		_____
12:00pm		_____
1:00		_____
2:00		_____
3:00		_____
4:00		_____
5:00		_____
6:00		_____
7:00		_____
8:00		_____
9:00		_____
10:00		_____

Essential Daily Planner for Men

DATE

☐ ☐ ☐ ☐ ☐ ☐ ☐
Mon Tues Wed Thu Fri Sat Sun

Appointment		Office

General plan		House

Reminder		

Time	Activity Description	Hobbies
12:00 am		
1:00		
2:00		
3:00		
4:00		
5:00		
6:00		
7:00		
8:00		
9:00		
10:00		
11:00		
12:00pm		
1:00		
2:00		
3:00		
4:00		
5:00		
6:00		
7:00		
8:00		
9:00		
10:00		

Essential Daily Planner for Men

DATE

☐ ☐ ☐ ☐ ☐ ☐ ☐

Mon Tues Wed Thu Fri Sat Sun

Appointment	**Office**

General plan	**House**

Reminder	

Time	Activity Description	**Hobbies**
12:00 am		
1:00		
2:00		
3:00		
4:00		
5:00		
6:00		
7:00		
8:00		
9:00		
10:00		
11:00		
12:00pm		
1:00		
2:00		
3:00		
4:00		
5:00		
6:00		
7:00		
8:00		
9:00		
10:00		

Essential Daily Planner for Men

DATE

☐ ☐ ☐ ☐ ☐ ☐ ☐
Mon Tues Wed Thu Fri Sat Sun

Appointment	**Office**

General plan	**House**

Reminder	

Time	Activity Description	**Hobbies**
12:00 am		
1:00		
2:00		
3:00		
4:00		
5:00		
6:00		
7:00		
8:00		
9:00		
10:00		
11:00		
12:00pm		
1:00		
2:00		
3:00		
4:00		
5:00		
6:00		
7:00		
8:00		
9:00		
10:00		

Essential Daily Planner for Men

DATE

☐ ☐ ☐ ☐ ☐ ☐ ☐
Mon Tues Wed Thu Fri Sat Sun

Appointment	Office

General plan	House

Reminder	

Time	Activity Description	Hobbies
12:00 am		
1:00		
2:00		
3:00		
4:00		
5:00		
6:00		
7:00		
8:00		
9:00		
10:00		
11:00		
12:00pm		
1:00		
2:00		
3:00		
4:00		
5:00		
6:00		
7:00		
8:00		
9:00		
10:00		

Essential Daily Planner for Men

DATE

☐ ☐ ☐ ☐ ☐ ☐ ☐
Mon Tues Wed Thu Fri Sat Sun

	Appointment		**Office**

	General plan		**House**

	Reminder		

Time	Activity Description	**Hobbies**
12:00 am		
1:00		
2:00		
3:00		
4:00		
5:00		
6:00		
7:00		
8:00		
9:00		
10:00		
11:00		
12:00pm		
1:00		
2:00		
3:00		
4:00		
5:00		
6:00		
7:00		
8:00		
9:00		
10:00		

Essential Daily Planner for Men

DATE

☐ ☐ ☐ ☐ ☐ ☐ ☐
Mon Tues Wed Thu Fri Sat Sun

Appointment		**Office**

General plan		**House**

Reminder		

Time	Activity Description	**Hobbies**
12:00 am		
1:00		
2:00		
3:00		
4:00		
5:00		
6:00		
7:00		
8:00		
9:00		
10:00		
11:00		
12:00pm		
1:00		
2:00		
3:00		
4:00		
5:00		
6:00		
7:00		
8:00		
9:00		
10:00		

Essential Daily Planner for Men

DATE

☐ ☐ ☐ ☐ ☐ ☐ ☐
Mon Tues Wed Thu Fri Sat Sun

Appointment

Office

General plan

House

Reminder

Time	Activity Description	Hobbies
12:00 am		
1:00		
2:00		
3:00		
4:00		
5:00		
6:00		
7:00		
8:00		
9:00		
10:00		
11:00		
12:00pm		
1:00		
2:00		
3:00		
4:00		
5:00		
6:00		
7:00		
8:00		
9:00		
10:00		

Essential Daily Planner for Men

DATE

☐ ☐ ☐ ☐ ☐ ☐ ☐
Mon Tues Wed Thu Fri Sat Sun

Appointment	**Office**

General plan	**House**

Reminder	

Time	Activity Description	**Hobbies**
12:00 am		
1:00		
2:00		
3:00		
4:00		
5:00		
6:00		
7:00		
8:00		
9:00		
10:00		
11:00		
12:00pm		
1:00		
2:00		
3:00		
4:00		
5:00		
6:00		
7:00		
8:00		
9:00		
10:00		

Essential Daily Planner for Men

DATE

☐ ☐ ☐ ☐ ☐ ☐ ☐
Mon Tues Wed Thu Fri Sat Sun

Appointment	**Office**

General plan	**House**

Reminder	

Time	Activity Description	**Hobbies**
12:00 am		
1:00		
2:00		
3:00		
4:00		
5:00		
6:00		
7:00		
8:00		
9:00		
10:00		
11:00		
12:00pm		
1:00		
2:00		
3:00		
4:00		
5:00		
6:00		
7:00		
8:00		
9:00		
10:00		

Essential Daily Planner for Men

DATE

☐ ☐ ☐ ☐ ☐ ☐ ☐
Mon Tues Wed Thu Fri Sat Sun

	Appointment		**Office**
	General plan		**House**
	Reminder		

Time	Activity Description	**Hobbies**
12:00 am		
1:00		
2:00		
3:00		
4:00		
5:00		
6:00		
7:00		
8:00		
9:00		
10:00		
11:00		
12:00pm		
1:00		
2:00		
3:00		
4:00		
5:00		
6:00		
7:00		
8:00		
9:00		
10:00		

Essential Daily Planner for Men

DATE

☐ ☐ ☐ ☐ ☐ ☐ ☐
Mon Tues Wed Thu Fri Sat Sun

Appointment

Office

General plan

House

Reminder

Time	Activity Description	Hobbies
12:00 am		
1:00		
2:00		
3:00		
4:00		
5:00		
6:00		
7:00		
8:00		
9:00		
10:00		
11:00		
12:00pm		
1:00		
2:00		
3:00		
4:00		
5:00		
6:00		
7:00		
8:00		
9:00		
10:00		

Essential Daily Planner for Men

DATE

☐ ☐ ☐ ☐ ☐ ☐ ☐
Mon Tues Wed Thu Fri Sat Sun

Appointment	**Office**

General plan	**House**

Reminder

Time	Activity Description	**Hobbies**
12:00 am		
1:00		
2:00		
3:00		
4:00		
5:00		
6:00		
7:00		
8:00		
9:00		
10:00		
11:00		
12:00pm		
1:00		
2:00		
3:00		
4:00		
5:00		
6:00		
7:00		
8:00		
9:00		
10:00		

Essential Daily Planner for Men

DATE

☐ ☐ ☐ ☐ ☐ ☐ ☐
Mon Tues Wed Thu Fri Sat Sun

Appointment		**Office**

General plan		**House**

Reminder		

Time	Activity Description	Hobbies
12:00 am		
1:00		
2:00		
3:00		
4:00		
5:00		
6:00		
7:00		
8:00		
9:00		
10:00		
11:00		
12:00pm		
1:00		
2:00		
3:00		
4:00		
5:00		
6:00		
7:00		
8:00		
9:00		
10:00		

Essential Daily Planner for Men

DATE

☐ ☐ ☐ ☐ ☐ ☐ ☐
Mon Tues Wed Thu Fri Sat Sun

Appointment		**Office**

General plan		**House**

Reminder		

Time	Activity Description	**Hobbies**
12:00 am		
1:00		
2:00		
3:00		
4:00		
5:00		
6:00		
7:00		
8:00		
9:00		
10:00		
11:00		
12:00pm		
1:00		
2:00		
3:00		
4:00		
5:00		
6:00		
7:00		
8:00		
9:00		
10:00		

Essential Daily Planner for Men

DATE

☐ ☐ ☐ ☐ ☐ ☐ ☐
Mon Tues Wed Thu Fri Sat Sun

Appointment		**Office**
_____		_____
_____		_____
_____		_____
_____		_____

General plan		**House**
_____		_____
_____		_____
_____		_____

Reminder		
_____		_____
_____		_____
_____		_____
_____		_____

Time	Activity Description	**Hobbies**
12:00 am		
1:00		
2:00		
3:00		
4:00		
5:00		
6:00		
7:00		
8:00		
9:00		
10:00		
11:00		
12:00pm		
1:00		
2:00		
3:00		
4:00		
5:00		
6:00		
7:00		
8:00		
9:00		
10:00		

Essential Daily Planner for Men

DATE

☐ ☐ ☐ ☐ ☐ ☐ ☐
Mon Tues Wed Thu Fri Sat Sun

Appointment	**Office**

General plan	**House**

Reminder	

Time	Activity Description	**Hobbies**
12:00 am		
1:00		
2:00		
3:00		
4:00		
5:00		
6:00		
7:00		
8:00		
9:00		
10:00		
11:00		
12:00pm		
1:00		
2:00		
3:00		
4:00		
5:00		
6:00		
7:00		
8:00		
9:00		
10:00		

Essential Daily Planner for Men

DATE

☐ ☐ ☐ ☐ ☐ ☐ ☐
Mon Tues Wed Thu Fri Sat Sun

Appointment		**Office**

_____
_____
_____
_____

| **General plan** | | **House** |

_____
_____
_____
_____

| **Reminder** |

_____
_____
_____
_____

Time	Activity Description	**Hobbies**
12:00 am		
1:00		
2:00		
3:00		
4:00		
5:00		
6:00		
7:00		
8:00		
9:00		
10:00		
11:00		
12:00pm		
1:00		
2:00		
3:00		
4:00		
5:00		
6:00		
7:00		
8:00		
9:00		
10:00		

Essential Daily Planner for Men

DATE

☐ ☐ ☐ ☐ ☐ ☐ ☐
Mon Tues Wed Thu Fri Sat Sun

Appointment	**Office**

General plan	**House**

Reminder	

Time	Activity Description	**Hobbies**
12:00 am		
1:00		
2:00		
3:00		
4:00		
5:00		
6:00		
7:00		
8:00		
9:00		
10:00		
11:00		
12:00pm		
1:00		
2:00		
3:00		
4:00		
5:00		
6:00		
7:00		
8:00		
9:00		
10:00		

Essential Daily Planner for Men

DATE

☐ ☐ ☐ ☐ ☐ ☐ ☐
Mon Tues Wed Thu Fri Sat Sun

	Appointment			Office

	General plan			House

	Reminder			

Time	Activity Description	Hobbies
12:00 am		
1:00		
2:00		
3:00		
4:00		
5:00		
6:00		
7:00		
8:00		
9:00		
10:00		
11:00		
12:00pm		
1:00		
2:00		
3:00		
4:00		
5:00		
6:00		
7:00		
8:00		
9:00		
10:00		

Essential Daily Planner for Men

DATE

☐ ☐ ☐ ☐ ☐ ☐ ☐
Mon Tues Wed Thu Fri Sat Sun

Appointment		**Office**

General plan		**House**

Reminder		

Time	Activity Description	**Hobbies**
12:00 am		
1:00		
2:00		
3:00		
4:00		
5:00		
6:00		
7:00		
8:00		
9:00		
10:00		
11:00		
12:00pm		
1:00		
2:00		
3:00		
4:00		
5:00		
6:00		
7:00		
8:00		
9:00		
10:00		

Essential Daily Planner for Men

DATE

☐ ☐ ☐ ☐ ☐ ☐ ☐
Mon Tues Wed Thu Fri Sat Sun

Appointment	**Office**

General plan	**House**

Reminder	

Time	Activity Description	**Hobbies**
12:00 am		
1:00		
2:00		
3:00		
4:00		
5:00		
6:00		
7:00		
8:00		
9:00		
10:00		
11:00		
12:00pm		
1:00		
2:00		
3:00		
4:00		
5:00		
6:00		
7:00		
8:00		
9:00		
10:00		

Essential Daily Planner for Men

DATE

☐ ☐ ☐ ☐ ☐ ☐ ☐
Mon Tues Wed Thu Fri Sat Sun

Appointment   **Office**

_____   _____
_____   _____
_____   _____
_____   _____

General plan   **House**

_____   _____
_____   _____
_____   _____
_____   _____

Reminder   _____

_____   _____
_____   _____
_____   _____

Time	Activity Description	**Hobbies**
12:00 am		
1:00		
2:00		
3:00		
4:00		
5:00		
6:00		
7:00		
8:00		
9:00		
10:00		
11:00		
12:00pm		
1:00		
2:00		
3:00		
4:00		
5:00		
6:00		
7:00		
8:00		
9:00		
10:00		

Essential Daily Planner for Men

DATE

☐ ☐ ☐ ☐ ☐ ☐ ☐
Mon Tues Wed Thu Fri Sat Sun

Appointment

Office

General plan

House

Reminder

Time	Activity Description	Hobbies
12:00 am		
1:00		
2:00		
3:00		
4:00		
5:00		
6:00		
7:00		
8:00		
9:00		
10:00		
11:00		
12:00pm		
1:00		
2:00		
3:00		
4:00		
5:00		
6:00		
7:00		
8:00		
9:00		
10:00		

Essential Daily Planner for Men

DATE

☐ ☐ ☐ ☐ ☐ ☐ ☐
Mon Tues Wed Thu Fri Sat Sun

Appointment

Office

General plan

House

Reminder

Time	Activity Description	**Hobbies**
12:00 am		
1:00		
2:00		
3:00		
4:00		
5:00		
6:00		
7:00		
8:00		
9:00		
10:00		
11:00		
12:00pm		
1:00		
2:00		
3:00		
4:00		
5:00		
6:00		
7:00		
8:00		
9:00		
10:00		

Essential Daily Planner for Men

DATE

☐ ☐ ☐ ☐ ☐ ☐ ☐
Mon Tues Wed Thu Fri Sat Sun

Appointment	**Office**

General plan	**House**

Reminder	

Time	Activity Description	**Hobbies**
12:00 am		
1:00		
2:00		
3:00		
4:00		
5:00		
6:00		
7:00		
8:00		
9:00		
10:00		
11:00		
12:00pm		
1:00		
2:00		
3:00		
4:00		
5:00		
6:00		
7:00		
8:00		
9:00		
10:00		

Essential Daily Planner for Men

DATE

☐ ☐ ☐ ☐ ☐ ☐ ☐
Mon Tues Wed Thu Fri Sat Sun

Appointment		**Office**

General plan		**House**

Reminder		

Time	Activity Description	**Hobbies**
12:00 am		
1:00		
2:00		
3:00		
4:00		
5:00		
6:00		
7:00		
8:00		
9:00		
10:00		
11:00		
12:00pm		
1:00		
2:00		
3:00		
4:00		
5:00		
6:00		
7:00		
8:00		
9:00		
10:00		

Essential Daily Planner for Men

DATE

☐ ☐ ☐ ☐ ☐ ☐ ☐
Mon Tues Wed Thu Fri Sat Sun

Appointment	**Office**

General plan	**House**

Reminder	

Time	Activity Description	**Hobbies**
12:00 am		
1:00		
2:00		
3:00		
4:00		
5:00		
6:00		
7:00		
8:00		
9:00		
10:00		
11:00		
12:00pm		
1:00		
2:00		
3:00		
4:00		
5:00		
6:00		
7:00		
8:00		
9:00		
10:00		

Essential Daily Planner for Men

DATE

☐ ☐ ☐ ☐ ☐ ☐ ☐
Mon Tues Wed Thu Fri Sat Sun

Appointment	**Office**

General plan	**House**

Reminder	

Time	Activity Description	**Hobbies**
12:00 am		
1:00		
2:00		
3:00		
4:00		
5:00		
6:00		
7:00		
8:00		
9:00		
10:00		
11:00		
12:00pm		
1:00		
2:00		
3:00		
4:00		
5:00		
6:00		
7:00		
8:00		
9:00		
10:00		

Essential Daily Planner for Men

DATE

☐ ☐ ☐ ☐ ☐ ☐ ☐
Mon Tues Wed Thu Fri Sat Sun

| **Appointment** | **Office** |

| **General plan** | **House** |

| **Reminder** |

Time	Activity Description	**Hobbies**
12:00 am		
1:00		
2:00		
3:00		
4:00		
5:00		
6:00		
7:00		
8:00		
9:00		
10:00		
11:00		
12:00pm		
1:00		
2:00		
3:00		
4:00		
5:00		
6:00		
7:00		
8:00		
9:00		
10:00		

Essential Daily Planner for Men

DATE

☐ ☐ ☐ ☐ ☐ ☐ ☐
Mon Tues Wed Thu Fri Sat Sun

	Appointment		**Office**

	General plan		**House**

	Reminder		

Time	Activity Description	**Hobbies**
12:00 am		
1:00		
2:00		
3:00		
4:00		
5:00		
6:00		
7:00		
8:00		
9:00		
10:00		
11:00		
12:00pm		
1:00		
2:00		
3:00		
4:00		
5:00		
6:00		
7:00		
8:00		
9:00		
10:00		

Essential Daily Planner for Men

DATE

☐ ☐ ☐ ☐ ☐ ☐ ☐
Mon Tues Wed Thu Fri Sat Sun

Appointment		**Office**

General plan		**House**

Reminder	

Time	Activity Description	**Hobbies**
12:00 am		
1:00		
2:00		
3:00		
4:00		
5:00		
6:00		
7:00		
8:00		
9:00		
10:00		
11:00		
12:00pm		
1:00		
2:00		
3:00		
4:00		
5:00		
6:00		
7:00		
8:00		
9:00		
10:00		

Essential Daily Planner for Men

DATE

☐ ☐ ☐ ☐ ☐ ☐ ☐
Mon Tues Wed Thu Fri Sat Sun

Appointment		**Office**

General plan		**House**

Reminder		

Time	Activity Description	**Hobbies**
12:00 am		
1:00		
2:00		
3:00		
4:00		
5:00		
6:00		
7:00		
8:00		
9:00		
10:00		
11:00		
12:00pm		
1:00		
2:00		
3:00		
4:00		
5:00		
6:00		
7:00		
8:00		
9:00		
10:00		

Essential Daily Planner for Men

DATE

☐ ☐ ☐ ☐ ☐ ☐ ☐
Mon Tues Wed Thu Fri Sat Sun

Appointment

Office

General plan

House

Reminder

Time	Activity Description	Hobbies
12:00 am		
1:00		
2:00		
3:00		
4:00		
5:00		
6:00		
7:00		
8:00		
9:00		
10:00		
11:00		
12:00pm		
1:00		
2:00		
3:00		
4:00		
5:00		
6:00		
7:00		
8:00		
9:00		
10:00		

Essential Daily Planner for Men

DATE

☐ ☐ ☐ ☐ ☐ ☐ ☐
Mon Tues Wed Thu Fri Sat Sun

	Appointment		**Office**
_____		_____	
_____		_____	
_____		_____	

	General plan		**House**
_____		_____	
_____		_____	
_____		_____	

	Reminder		
_____		_____	
_____		_____	
_____		_____	

Time	Activity Description	**Hobbies**
12:00 am		
1:00		
2:00		
3:00		
4:00		
5:00		
6:00		
7:00		
8:00		
9:00		
10:00		
11:00		
12:00pm		
1:00		
2:00		
3:00		
4:00		
5:00		
6:00		
7:00		
8:00		
9:00		
10:00		

Essential Daily Planner for Men

DATE

☐ ☐ ☐ ☐ ☐ ☐ ☐

Mon Tues Wed Thu Fri Sat Sun

Appointment	**Office**

General plan	**House**

Reminder	

Time	Activity Description	**Hobbies**
12:00 am		
1:00		
2:00		
3:00		
4:00		
5:00		
6:00		
7:00		
8:00		
9:00		
10:00		
11:00		
12:00pm		
1:00		
2:00		
3:00		
4:00		
5:00		
6:00		
7:00		
8:00		
9:00		
10:00		

Essential Daily Planner for Men

DATE

☐ ☐ ☐ ☐ ☐ ☐ ☐
Mon Tues Wed Thu Fri Sat Sun

Appointment		**Office**

General plan		**House**

Reminder		

Time	Activity Description	**Hobbies**
12:00 am		
1:00		
2:00		
3:00		
4:00		
5:00		
6:00		
7:00		
8:00		
9:00		
10:00		
11:00		
12:00pm		
1:00		
2:00		
3:00		
4:00		
5:00		
6:00		
7:00		
8:00		
9:00		
10:00		

Essential Daily Planner for Men

DATE

☐ ☐ ☐ ☐ ☐ ☐ ☐
Mon Tues Wed Thu Fri Sat Sun

Appointment

_____
_____
_____
_____

Office

_____
_____
_____
_____

General plan

_____
_____
_____

House

_____
_____
_____

Reminder

_____
_____
_____
_____

Time	Activity Description
12:00 am	
1:00	
2:00	
3:00	
4:00	
5:00	
6:00	
7:00	
8:00	
9:00	
10:00	
11:00	
12:00pm	
1:00	
2:00	
3:00	
4:00	
5:00	
6:00	
7:00	
8:00	
9:00	
10:00	

Hobbies

_____
_____
_____
_____
_____
_____
_____
_____
_____
_____
_____
_____
_____
_____

Essential Daily Planner for Men

DATE

☐ ☐ ☐ ☐ ☐ ☐ ☐
Mon Tues Wed Thu Fri Sat Sun

Appointment

Office

General plan

House

Reminder

Time	Activity Description	**Hobbies**
12:00 am		
1:00		
2:00		
3:00		
4:00		
5:00		
6:00		
7:00		
8:00		
9:00		
10:00		
11:00		
12:00pm		
1:00		
2:00		
3:00		
4:00		
5:00		
6:00		
7:00		
8:00		
9:00		
10:00		

Essential Daily Planner for Men

DATE

☐ ☐ ☐ ☐ ☐ ☐ ☐
Mon Tues Wed Thu Fri Sat Sun

Appointment	**Office**

General plan	**House**

Reminder	

Time	Activity Description	**Hobbies**
12:00 am		
1:00		
2:00		
3:00		
4:00		
5:00		
6:00		
7:00		
8:00		
9:00		
10:00		
11:00		
12:00pm		
1:00		
2:00		
3:00		
4:00		
5:00		
6:00		
7:00		
8:00		
9:00		
10:00		

Essential Daily Planner for Men

DATE

☐ ☐ ☐ ☐ ☐ ☐ ☐
Mon Tues Wed Thu Fri Sat Sun

Appointment		**Office**

General plan		**House**

Reminder		

Time	Activity Description	Hobbies
12:00 am		
1:00		
2:00		
3:00		
4:00		
5:00		
6:00		
7:00		
8:00		
9:00		
10:00		
11:00		
12:00pm		
1:00		
2:00		
3:00		
4:00		
5:00		
6:00		
7:00		
8:00		
9:00		
10:00		

Essential Daily Planner for Men

DATE

☐ ☐ ☐ ☐ ☐ ☐ ☐
Mon Tues Wed Thu Fri Sat Sun

Appointment		**Office**

General plan		**House**

Reminder	

Time	Activity Description	**Hobbies**
12:00 am		
1:00		
2:00		
3:00		
4:00		
5:00		
6:00		
7:00		
8:00		
9:00		
10:00		
11:00		
12:00pm		
1:00		
2:00		
3:00		
4:00		
5:00		
6:00		
7:00		
8:00		
9:00		
10:00		

Essential Daily Planner for Men

DATE

☐ ☐ ☐ ☐ ☐ ☐ ☐
Mon Tues Wed Thu Fri Sat Sun

Appointment	**Office**

General plan	**House**

Reminder	

Time	Activity Description	**Hobbies**
12:00 am		
1:00		
2:00		
3:00		
4:00		
5:00		
6:00		
7:00		
8:00		
9:00		
10:00		
11:00		
12:00pm		
1:00		
2:00		
3:00		
4:00		
5:00		
6:00		
7:00		
8:00		
9:00		
10:00		

Essential Daily Planner for Men

DATE

☐ ☐ ☐ ☐ ☐ ☐ ☐
Mon Tues Wed Thu Fri Sat Sun

	Appointment		**Office**

	General plan		**House**

	Reminder		

Time	Activity Description	**Hobbies**
12:00 am		
1:00		
2:00		
3:00		
4:00		
5:00		
6:00		
7:00		
8:00		
9:00		
10:00		
11:00		
12:00pm		
1:00		
2:00		
3:00		
4:00		
5:00		
6:00		
7:00		
8:00		
9:00		
10:00		

Essential Daily Planner for Men

DATE

☐ ☐ ☐ ☐ ☐ ☐ ☐
Mon Tues Wed Thu Fri Sat Sun

Appointment

Office

General plan

House

Reminder

Time	Activity Description	**Hobbies**
12:00 am		
1:00		
2:00		
3:00		
4:00		
5:00		
6:00		
7:00		
8:00		
9:00		
10:00		
11:00		
12:00pm		
1:00		
2:00		
3:00		
4:00		
5:00		
6:00		
7:00		
8:00		
9:00		
10:00		

Essential Daily Planner for Men

DATE

☐ ☐ ☐ ☐ ☐ ☐ ☐
Mon Tues Wed Thu Fri Sat Sun

Appointment	**Office**

General plan	**House**

Reminder	

Time	Activity Description	Hobbies
12:00 am		
1:00		
2:00		
3:00		
4:00		
5:00		
6:00		
7:00		
8:00		
9:00		
10:00		
11:00		
12:00pm		
1:00		
2:00		
3:00		
4:00		
5:00		
6:00		
7:00		
8:00		
9:00		
10:00		

Essential Daily Planner for Men

DATE

☐ ☐ ☐ ☐ ☐ ☐ ☐

Mon Tues Wed Thu Fri Sat Sun

Appointment	**Office**

General plan	**House**

Reminder	

Time	Activity Description	**Hobbies**
12:00 am		
1:00		
2:00		
3:00		
4:00		
5:00		
6:00		
7:00		
8:00		
9:00		
10:00		
11:00		
12:00pm		
1:00		
2:00		
3:00		
4:00		
5:00		
6:00		
7:00		
8:00		
9:00		
10:00		

Essential Daily Planner for Men

DATE

☐ ☐ ☐ ☐ ☐ ☐ ☐
Mon Tues Wed Thu Fri Sat Sun

Appointment	**Office**
_____	_____
_____	_____
_____	_____

General plan	**House**
_____	_____
_____	_____
_____	_____

Reminder	
_____	_____
_____	_____
_____	_____

Time	Activity Description	**Hobbies**
12:00 am		_____
1:00		_____
2:00		_____
3:00		_____
4:00		_____
5:00		_____
6:00		_____
7:00		_____
8:00		_____
9:00		_____
10:00		_____
11:00		_____
12:00pm		_____
1:00		_____
2:00		_____
3:00		_____
4:00		_____
5:00		_____
6:00		_____
7:00		_____
8:00		_____
9:00		_____
10:00		_____

Essential Daily Planner for Men

DATE

☐ ☐ ☐ ☐ ☐ ☐ ☐
Mon Tues Wed Thu Fri Sat Sun

	Appointment		**Office**

	General plan		**House**

	Reminder		

Time	Activity Description		**Hobbies**
12:00 am			
1:00			
2:00			
3:00			
4:00			
5:00			
6:00			
7:00			
8:00			
9:00			
10:00			
11:00			
12:00pm			
1:00			
2:00			
3:00			
4:00			
5:00			
6:00			
7:00			
8:00			
9:00			
10:00			

Essential Daily Planner for Men

DATE

☐ ☐ ☐ ☐ ☐ ☐ ☐
Mon Tues Wed Thu Fri Sat Sun

Appointment	**Office**

General plan	**House**

Reminder	

Time	Activity Description	**Hobbies**
12:00 am		
1:00		
2:00		
3:00		
4:00		
5:00		
6:00		
7:00		
8:00		
9:00		
10:00		
11:00		
12:00pm		
1:00		
2:00		
3:00		
4:00		
5:00		
6:00		
7:00		
8:00		
9:00		
10:00		

Essential Daily Planner for Men

DATE

☐ ☐ ☐ ☐ ☐ ☐ ☐
Mon Tues Wed Thu Fri Sat Sun

	Appointment		**Office**

	General plan		**House**

	Reminder		

Time	Activity Description		**Hobbies**
12:00 am			
1:00			
2:00			
3:00			
4:00			
5:00			
6:00			
7:00			
8:00			
9:00			
10:00			
11:00			
12:00pm			
1:00			
2:00			
3:00			
4:00			
5:00			
6:00			
7:00			
8:00			
9:00			
10:00			

Essential Daily Planner for Men

DATE

☐ ☐ ☐ ☐ ☐ ☐ ☐

Mon Tues Wed Thu Fri Sat Sun

	Appointment		**Office**

	General plan		**House**

	Reminder		

Time	Activity Description		**Hobbies**
12:00 am			
1:00			
2:00			
3:00			
4:00			
5:00			
6:00			
7:00			
8:00			
9:00			
10:00			
11:00			
12:00pm			
1:00			
2:00			
3:00			
4:00			
5:00			
6:00			
7:00			
8:00			
9:00			
10:00			

Essential Daily Planner for Men

DATE

☐ ☐ ☐ ☐ ☐ ☐ ☐
Mon Tues Wed Thu Fri Sat Sun

Appointment		Office
_____		_____
_____		_____
_____		_____
_____		_____

General plan		House
_____		_____
_____		_____
_____		_____

Reminder		
_____		_____
_____		_____
_____		_____

Time	Activity Description	Hobbies
12:00 am		_____
1:00		_____
2:00		_____
3:00		_____
4:00		_____
5:00		_____
6:00		_____
7:00		_____
8:00		_____
9:00		_____
10:00		_____
11:00		_____
12:00pm		_____
1:00		_____
2:00		_____
3:00		_____
4:00		_____
5:00		_____
6:00		_____
7:00		_____
8:00		_____
9:00		_____
10:00		_____

Essential Daily Planner for Men

DATE

☐ ☐ ☐ ☐ ☐ ☐ ☐
Mon Tues Wed Thu Fri Sat Sun

Appointment		**Office**

General plan		**House**

Reminder		

Time	Activity Description	Hobbies
12:00 am		
1:00		
2:00		
3:00		
4:00		
5:00		
6:00		
7:00		
8:00		
9:00		
10:00		
11:00		
12:00pm		
1:00		
2:00		
3:00		
4:00		
5:00		
6:00		
7:00		
8:00		
9:00		
10:00		

Essential Daily Planner for Men

DATE

☐ ☐ ☐ ☐ ☐ ☐ ☐
Mon Tues Wed Thu Fri Sat Sun

Appointment

Office

General plan

House

Reminder

Time	Activity Description	Hobbies
12:00 am		
1:00		
2:00		
3:00		
4:00		
5:00		
6:00		
7:00		
8:00		
9:00		
10:00		
11:00		
12:00pm		
1:00		
2:00		
3:00		
4:00		
5:00		
6:00		
7:00		
8:00		
9:00		
10:00		

Essential Daily Planner for Men

DATE

☐ ☐ ☐ ☐ ☐ ☐ ☐
Mon Tues Wed Thu Fri Sat Sun

Appointment	**Office**

General plan	**House**

Reminder	

Time	Activity Description	**Hobbies**
12:00 am		
1:00		
2:00		
3:00		
4:00		
5:00		
6:00		
7:00		
8:00		
9:00		
10:00		
11:00		
12:00pm		
1:00		
2:00		
3:00		
4:00		
5:00		
6:00		
7:00		
8:00		
9:00		
10:00		

Essential Daily Planner for Men

DATE

☐ ☐ ☐ ☐ ☐ ☐ ☐
Mon Tues Wed Thu Fri Sat Sun

Appointment   **Office**

_____   _____
_____   _____
_____   _____
_____   _____

General plan   **House**

_____   _____
_____   _____
_____   _____
_____   _____

Reminder

_____   _____
_____   _____
_____   _____
_____   _____

Time	Activity Description	**Hobbies**
12:00 am		_____
1:00		_____
2:00		_____
3:00		_____
4:00		_____
5:00		_____
6:00		_____
7:00		_____
8:00		_____
9:00		_____
10:00		_____
11:00		_____
12:00pm		_____
1:00		_____
2:00		_____
3:00		_____
4:00		_____
5:00		_____
6:00		_____
7:00		_____
8:00		_____
9:00		_____
10:00		_____

Essential Daily Planner for Men

DATE

☐ ☐ ☐ ☐ ☐ ☐ ☐
Mon Tues Wed Thu Fri Sat Sun

Appointment	**Office**

General plan	**House**

Reminder	

Time	Activity Description	**Hobbies**
12:00 am		
1:00		
2:00		
3:00		
4:00		
5:00		
6:00		
7:00		
8:00		
9:00		
10:00		
11:00		
12:00pm		
1:00		
2:00		
3:00		
4:00		
5:00		
6:00		
7:00		
8:00		
9:00		
10:00		

Essential Daily Planner for Men

DATE

☐ ☐ ☐ ☐ ☐ ☐ ☐

Mon Tues Wed Thu Fri Sat Sun

	Appointment		**Office**

	General plan		**House**

	Reminder		

Time	Activity Description	**Hobbies**
12:00 am		
1:00		
2:00		
3:00		
4:00		
5:00		
6:00		
7:00		
8:00		
9:00		
10:00		
11:00		
12:00pm		
1:00		
2:00		
3:00		
4:00		
5:00		
6:00		
7:00		
8:00		
9:00		
10:00		

Essential Daily Planner for Men

DATE

☐ ☐ ☐ ☐ ☐ ☐ ☐
Mon Tues Wed Thu Fri Sat Sun

Appointment	**Office**

General plan	**House**

Reminder	

Time	Activity Description	**Hobbies**
12:00 am		
1:00		
2:00		
3:00		
4:00		
5:00		
6:00		
7:00		
8:00		
9:00		
10:00		
11:00		
12:00pm		
1:00		
2:00		
3:00		
4:00		
5:00		
6:00		
7:00		
8:00		
9:00		
10:00		

Essential Daily Planner for Men

DATE

☐ ☐ ☐ ☐ ☐ ☐ ☐
Mon Tues Wed Thu Fri Sat Sun

Appointment

Office

General plan

House

Reminder

Time	Activity Description	Hobbies
12:00 am		
1:00		
2:00		
3:00		
4:00		
5:00		
6:00		
7:00		
8:00		
9:00		
10:00		
11:00		
12:00pm		
1:00		
2:00		
3:00		
4:00		
5:00		
6:00		
7:00		
8:00		
9:00		
10:00		

Essential Daily Planner for Men

DATE

☐ ☐ ☐ ☐ ☐ ☐ ☐
Mon Tues Wed Thu Fri Sat Sun

Appointment	Office

General plan	House

Reminder	

Time	Activity Description	Hobbies
12:00 am		
1:00		
2:00		
3:00		
4:00		
5:00		
6:00		
7:00		
8:00		
9:00		
10:00		
11:00		
12:00pm		
1:00		
2:00		
3:00		
4:00		
5:00		
6:00		
7:00		
8:00		
9:00		
10:00		

Essential Daily Planner for Men

DATE

☐ ☐ ☐ ☐ ☐ ☐ ☐
Mon Tues Wed Thu Fri Sat Sun

Appointment

Office

General plan

House

Reminder

Time	Activity Description	**Hobbies**
12:00 am		
1:00		
2:00		
3:00		
4:00		
5:00		
6:00		
7:00		
8:00		
9:00		
10:00		
11:00		
12:00pm		
1:00		
2:00		
3:00		
4:00		
5:00		
6:00		
7:00		
8:00		
9:00		
10:00		

Essential Daily Planner for Men

DATE

☐ ☐ ☐ ☐ ☐ ☐ ☐
Mon Tues Wed Thu Fri Sat Sun

	Appointment		**Office**
_____		_____	
_____		_____	
_____		_____	

	General plan		**House**
_____		_____	
_____		_____	
_____		_____	

	Reminder		
_____		_____	
_____		_____	
_____		_____	

Time	Activity Description	**Hobbies**
12:00 am		
1:00		
2:00		
3:00		
4:00		
5:00		
6:00		
7:00		
8:00		
9:00		
10:00		
11:00		
12:00pm		
1:00		
2:00		
3:00		
4:00		
5:00		
6:00		
7:00		
8:00		
9:00		
10:00		

Essential Daily Planner for Men

DATE

☐ ☐ ☐ ☐ ☐ ☐ ☐
Mon Tues Wed Thu Fri Sat Sun

Appointment

Office

General plan

House

Reminder

Time	Activity Description	**Hobbies**
12:00 am		
1:00		
2:00		
3:00		
4:00		
5:00		
6:00		
7:00		
8:00		
9:00		
10:00		
11:00		
12:00pm		
1:00		
2:00		
3:00		
4:00		
5:00		
6:00		
7:00		
8:00		
9:00		
10:00		

Essential Daily Planner for Men

DATE

☐ ☐ ☐ ☐ ☐ ☐ ☐
Mon Tues Wed Thu Fri Sat Sun

Appointment	**Office**

General plan	**House**

Reminder	

Time	Activity Description	**Hobbies**
12:00 am		
1:00		
2:00		
3:00		
4:00		
5:00		
6:00		
7:00		
8:00		
9:00		
10:00		
11:00		
12:00pm		
1:00		
2:00		
3:00		
4:00		
5:00		
6:00		
7:00		
8:00		
9:00		
10:00		

Essential Daily Planner for Men

DATE

☐ ☐ ☐ ☐ ☐ ☐ ☐
Mon Tues Wed Thu Fri Sat Sun

Appointment

Office

General plan

House

Reminder

Time	Activity Description	**Hobbies**
12:00 am		
1:00		
2:00		
3:00		
4:00		
5:00		
6:00		
7:00		
8:00		
9:00		
10:00		
11:00		
12:00pm		
1:00		
2:00		
3:00		
4:00		
5:00		
6:00		
7:00		
8:00		
9:00		
10:00		

Essential Daily Planner for Men

DATE

☐ ☐ ☐ ☐ ☐ ☐ ☐
Mon Tues Wed Thu Fri Sat Sun

	Appointment		**Office**
_____		_____	
_____		_____	
_____		_____	

	General plan		**House**
_____		_____	
_____		_____	
_____		_____	

	Reminder		
_____		_____	
_____		_____	
_____		_____	

Time	Activity Description	**Hobbies**
12:00 am		
1:00		
2:00		
3:00		
4:00		
5:00		
6:00		
7:00		
8:00		
9:00		
10:00		
11:00		
12:00pm		
1:00		
2:00		
3:00		
4:00		
5:00		
6:00		
7:00		
8:00		
9:00		
10:00		

Essential Daily Planner for Men

DATE

☐ ☐ ☐ ☐ ☐ ☐ ☐
Mon Tues Wed Thu Fri Sat Sun

Appointment	**Office**

General plan	**House**

Reminder	

Time	Activity Description	**Hobbies**
12:00 am		
1:00		
2:00		
3:00		
4:00		
5:00		
6:00		
7:00		
8:00		
9:00		
10:00		
11:00		
12:00pm		
1:00		
2:00		
3:00		
4:00		
5:00		
6:00		
7:00		
8:00		
9:00		
10:00		

Essential Daily Planner for Men

DATE

☐ ☐ ☐ ☐ ☐ ☐ ☐
Mon Tues Wed Thu Fri Sat Sun

| **Appointment** | **Office** |

_____
_____
_____

| **General plan** | **House** |

_____
_____
_____

| **Reminder** |

_____
_____
_____

Time	Activity Description	**Hobbies**
12:00 am		
1:00		
2:00		
3:00		
4:00		
5:00		
6:00		
7:00		
8:00		
9:00		
10:00		
11:00		
12:00pm		
1:00		
2:00		
3:00		
4:00		
5:00		
6:00		
7:00		
8:00		
9:00		
10:00		

Essential Daily Planner for Men

DATE

☐ ☐ ☐ ☐ ☐ ☐ ☐
Mon Tues Wed Thu Fri Sat Sun

Appointment

Office

General plan

House

Reminder

Time	Activity Description	Hobbies
12:00 am		
1:00		
2:00		
3:00		
4:00		
5:00		
6:00		
7:00		
8:00		
9:00		
10:00		
11:00		
12:00pm		
1:00		
2:00		
3:00		
4:00		
5:00		
6:00		
7:00		
8:00		
9:00		
10:00		

Essential Daily Planner for Men

DATE

☐ ☐ ☐ ☐ ☐ ☐ ☐
Mon Tues Wed Thu Fri Sat Sun

Appointment	**Office**

General plan	**House**

Reminder	

Time	Activity Description	**Hobbies**
12:00 am		
1:00		
2:00		
3:00		
4:00		
5:00		
6:00		
7:00		
8:00		
9:00		
10:00		
11:00		
12:00pm		
1:00		
2:00		
3:00		
4:00		
5:00		
6:00		
7:00		
8:00		
9:00		
10:00		

Essential Daily Planner for Men

DATE

☐ ☐ ☐ ☐ ☐ ☐ ☐
Mon Tues Wed Thu Fri Sat Sun

Appointment

_____
_____
_____
_____

General plan

_____
_____
_____
_____

Reminder

_____
_____
_____
_____

Office

_____
_____
_____

House

_____
_____
_____
_____

Time	Activity Description
12:00 am	
1:00	
2:00	
3:00	
4:00	
5:00	
6:00	
7:00	
8:00	
9:00	
10:00	
11:00	
12:00pm	
1:00	
2:00	
3:00	
4:00	
5:00	
6:00	
7:00	
8:00	
9:00	
10:00	

Hobbies

_____
_____
_____
_____
_____
_____
_____
_____
_____
_____
_____
_____
_____
_____
_____

Essential Daily Planner for Men

DATE

☐ ☐ ☐ ☐ ☐ ☐ ☐
Mon Tues Wed Thu Fri Sat Sun

Appointment

Office

General plan

House

Reminder

Time	Activity Description	Hobbies
12:00 am		
1:00		
2:00		
3:00		
4:00		
5:00		
6:00		
7:00		
8:00		
9:00		
10:00		
11:00		
12:00pm		
1:00		
2:00		
3:00		
4:00		
5:00		
6:00		
7:00		
8:00		
9:00		
10:00		

Essential Daily Planner for Men

DATE

☐ ☐ ☐ ☐ ☐ ☐ ☐

Mon Tues Wed Thu Fri Sat Sun

Appointment		**Office**

General plan		**House**

Reminder		

Time	Activity Description	**Hobbies**
12:00 am		
1:00		
2:00		
3:00		
4:00		
5:00		
6:00		
7:00		
8:00		
9:00		
10:00		
11:00		
12:00pm		
1:00		
2:00		
3:00		
4:00		
5:00		
6:00		
7:00		
8:00		
9:00		
10:00		

Essential Daily Planner for Men

DATE

☐ ☐ ☐ ☐ ☐ ☐ ☐
Mon Tues Wed Thu Fri Sat Sun

Appointment	**Office**

General plan	**House**

Reminder	

Time	Activity Description	**Hobbies**
12:00 am		
1:00		
2:00		
3:00		
4:00		
5:00		
6:00		
7:00		
8:00		
9:00		
10:00		
11:00		
12:00pm		
1:00		
2:00		
3:00		
4:00		
5:00		
6:00		
7:00		
8:00		
9:00		
10:00		

Essential Daily Planner for Men

DATE

☐ ☐ ☐ ☐ ☐ ☐ ☐
Mon Tues Wed Thu Fri Sat Sun

Appointment

Office

General plan

House

Reminder

Time	Activity Description	Hobbies
12:00 am		
1:00		
2:00		
3:00		
4:00		
5:00		
6:00		
7:00		
8:00		
9:00		
10:00		
11:00		
12:00pm		
1:00		
2:00		
3:00		
4:00		
5:00		
6:00		
7:00		
8:00		
9:00		
10:00		

Essential Daily Planner for Men

DATE

☐ ☐ ☐ ☐ ☐ ☐ ☐
Mon Tues Wed Thu Fri Sat Sun

Appointment		**Office**

General plan		**House**

Reminder		

Time	Activity Description	**Hobbies**
12:00 am		
1:00		
2:00		
3:00		
4:00		
5:00		
6:00		
7:00		
8:00		
9:00		
10:00		
11:00		
12:00pm		
1:00		
2:00		
3:00		
4:00		
5:00		
6:00		
7:00		
8:00		
9:00		
10:00		

Essential Daily Planner for Men

DATE

☐ ☐ ☐ ☐ ☐ ☐ ☐
Mon Tues Wed Thu Fri Sat Sun

Appointment

Office

General plan

House

Reminder

Time	Activity Description	Hobbies
12:00 am		
1:00		
2:00		
3:00		
4:00		
5:00		
6:00		
7:00		
8:00		
9:00		
10:00		
11:00		
12:00pm		
1:00		
2:00		
3:00		
4:00		
5:00		
6:00		
7:00		
8:00		
9:00		
10:00		

Essential Daily Planner for Men

DATE

☐ ☐ ☐ ☐ ☐ ☐ ☐
Mon Tues Wed Thu Fri Sat Sun

Appointment	**Office**
_____	_____
_____	_____
_____	_____

General plan	**House**
_____	_____
_____	_____
_____	_____

Reminder	
_____	_____
_____	_____
_____	_____

Time	Activity Description	**Hobbies**
12:00 am		
1:00		
2:00		
3:00		
4:00		
5:00		
6:00		
7:00		
8:00		
9:00		
10:00		
11:00		
12:00pm		
1:00		
2:00		
3:00		
4:00		
5:00		
6:00		
7:00		
8:00		
9:00		
10:00		

Essential Daily Planner for Men

DATE

☐ ☐ ☐ ☐ ☐ ☐ ☐
Mon Tues Wed Thu Fri Sat Sun

Appointment

Office

General plan

House

Reminder

Time	Activity Description
12:00 am	
1:00	
2:00	
3:00	
4:00	
5:00	
6:00	
7:00	
8:00	
9:00	
10:00	
11:00	
12:00pm	
1:00	
2:00	
3:00	
4:00	
5:00	
6:00	
7:00	
8:00	
9:00	
10:00	

Hobbies

Essential Daily Planner for Men

DATE

☐ ☐ ☐ ☐ ☐ ☐ ☐
Mon Tues Wed Thu Fri Sat Sun

Appointment	**Office**

General plan	**House**

Reminder

Time	Activity Description	**Hobbies**
12:00 am		
1:00		
2:00		
3:00		
4:00		
5:00		
6:00		
7:00		
8:00		
9:00		
10:00		
11:00		
12:00pm		
1:00		
2:00		
3:00		
4:00		
5:00		
6:00		
7:00		
8:00		
9:00		
10:00		

Essential Daily Planner for Men

DATE

☐ ☐ ☐ ☐ ☐ ☐ ☐
Mon Tues Wed Thu Fri Sat Sun

Appointment	**Office**

General plan	**House**

Reminder	

Time	Activity Description	**Hobbies**
12:00 am		
1:00		
2:00		
3:00		
4:00		
5:00		
6:00		
7:00		
8:00		
9:00		
10:00		
11:00		
12:00pm		
1:00		
2:00		
3:00		
4:00		
5:00		
6:00		
7:00		
8:00		
9:00		
10:00		

Essential Daily Planner for Men

DATE

☐ ☐ ☐ ☐ ☐ ☐ ☐
Mon Tues Wed Thu Fri Sat Sun

Appointment	**Office**
General plan	**House**
Reminder	

Time	Activity Description	Hobbies
12:00 am		
1:00		
2:00		
3:00		
4:00		
5:00		
6:00		
7:00		
8:00		
9:00		
10:00		
11:00		
12:00pm		
1:00		
2:00		
3:00		
4:00		
5:00		
6:00		
7:00		
8:00		
9:00		
10:00		

Essential Daily Planner for Men

DATE

☐ ☐ ☐ ☐ ☐ ☐ ☐
Mon Tues Wed Thu Fri Sat Sun

Appointment   **Office**

_____   _____
_____   _____
_____   _____
_____   _____

General plan   **House**

_____   _____
_____   _____
_____   _____
_____   _____

Reminder   _____

_____   _____
_____   _____
_____   _____

Time	Activity Description	**Hobbies**
12:00 am		
1:00		
2:00		
3:00		
4:00		
5:00		
6:00		
7:00		
8:00		
9:00		
10:00		
11:00		
12:00pm		
1:00		
2:00		
3:00		
4:00		
5:00		
6:00		
7:00		
8:00		
9:00		
10:00		

Essential Daily Planner for Men

DATE

☐ ☐ ☐ ☐ ☐ ☐ ☐
Mon Tues Wed Thu Fri Sat Sun

Appointment	**Office**
_____	_____
_____	_____
_____	_____

General plan	**House**
_____	_____
_____	_____
_____	_____

Reminder	
_____	_____
_____	_____
_____	_____

Time	Activity Description	**Hobbies**
12:00 am		_____
1:00		_____
2:00		_____
3:00		_____
4:00		_____
5:00		_____
6:00		_____
7:00		_____
8:00		_____
9:00		_____
10:00		_____
11:00		_____
12:00pm		_____
1:00		_____
2:00		_____
3:00		_____
4:00		_____
5:00		_____
6:00		_____
7:00		_____
8:00		_____
9:00		_____
10:00		_____

Essential Daily Planner for Men

DATE

☐ ☐ ☐ ☐ ☐ ☐ ☐
Mon Tues Wed Thu Fri Sat Sun

Appointment

Office

General plan

House

Reminder

Time	Activity Description	Hobbies
12:00 am		
1:00		
2:00		
3:00		
4:00		
5:00		
6:00		
7:00		
8:00		
9:00		
10:00		
11:00		
12:00pm		
1:00		
2:00		
3:00		
4:00		
5:00		
6:00		
7:00		
8:00		
9:00		
10:00		

Essential Daily Planner for Men

DATE

☐ ☐ ☐ ☐ ☐ ☐ ☐
Mon Tues Wed Thu Fri Sat Sun

Appointment	**Office**

General plan	**House**

Reminder	

Time	Activity Description	**Hobbies**
12:00 am		
1:00		
2:00		
3:00		
4:00		
5:00		
6:00		
7:00		
8:00		
9:00		
10:00		
11:00		
12:00pm		
1:00		
2:00		
3:00		
4:00		
5:00		
6:00		
7:00		
8:00		
9:00		
10:00		

Essential Daily Planner for Men

DATE

☐ ☐ ☐ ☐ ☐ ☐ ☐
Mon Tues Wed Thu Fri Sat Sun

Appointment

Office

General plan

House

Reminder

Time	Activity Description		**Hobbies**
12:00 am			
1:00			
2:00			
3:00			
4:00			
5:00			
6:00			
7:00			
8:00			
9:00			
10:00			
11:00			
12:00pm			
1:00			
2:00			
3:00			
4:00			
5:00			
6:00			
7:00			
8:00			
9:00			
10:00			

Essential Daily Planner for Men

DATE

☐ ☐ ☐ ☐ ☐ ☐ ☐
Mon Tues Wed Thu Fri Sat Sun

Appointment

Office

General plan

House

Reminder

Time	Activity Description	Hobbies
12:00 am		
1:00		
2:00		
3:00		
4:00		
5:00		
6:00		
7:00		
8:00		
9:00		
10:00		
11:00		
12:00pm		
1:00		
2:00		
3:00		
4:00		
5:00		
6:00		
7:00		
8:00		
9:00		
10:00		

Essential Daily Planner for Men

DATE

☐ ☐ ☐ ☐ ☐ ☐ ☐
Mon Tues Wed Thu Fri Sat Sun

Appointment

Office

General plan

House

Reminder

Time	Activity Description	**Hobbies**
12:00 am		
1:00		
2:00		
3:00		
4:00		
5:00		
6:00		
7:00		
8:00		
9:00		
10:00		
11:00		
12:00pm		
1:00		
2:00		
3:00		
4:00		
5:00		
6:00		
7:00		
8:00		
9:00		
10:00		

Essential Daily Planner for Men

DATE

☐ ☐ ☐ ☐ ☐ ☐ ☐
Mon Tues Wed Thu Fri Sat Sun

Appointment	**Office**

General plan	**House**

Reminder	

Time	Activity Description	**Hobbies**
12:00 am		
1:00		
2:00		
3:00		
4:00		
5:00		
6:00		
7:00		
8:00		
9:00		
10:00		
11:00		
12:00pm		
1:00		
2:00		
3:00		
4:00		
5:00		
6:00		
7:00		
8:00		
9:00		
10:00		

Essential Daily Planner for Men

DATE

☐ ☐ ☐ ☐ ☐ ☐ ☐
Mon Tues Wed Thu Fri Sat Sun

		Appointment		**Office**

		General plan		**House**

		Reminder		

Time	Activity Description	Hobbies
12:00 am		
1:00		
2:00		
3:00		
4:00		
5:00		
6:00		
7:00		
8:00		
9:00		
10:00		
11:00		
12:00pm		
1:00		
2:00		
3:00		
4:00		
5:00		
6:00		
7:00		
8:00		
9:00		
10:00		

Essential Daily Planner for Men

DATE

☐ ☐ ☐ ☐ ☐ ☐ ☐
Mon Tues Wed Thu Fri Sat Sun

| **Appointment** | **Office** |

| **General plan** | **House** |

| **Reminder** | |

Time	Activity Description	**Hobbies**
12:00 am		
1:00		
2:00		
3:00		
4:00		
5:00		
6:00		
7:00		
8:00		
9:00		
10:00		
11:00		
12:00pm		
1:00		
2:00		
3:00		
4:00		
5:00		
6:00		
7:00		
8:00		
9:00		
10:00		

Essential Daily Planner for Men

DATE

☐ ☐ ☐ ☐ ☐ ☐ ☐
Mon Tues Wed Thu Fri Sat Sun

Appointment	**Office**

General plan	**House**

Reminder	

Time	Activity Description	**Hobbies**
12:00 am		
1:00		
2:00		
3:00		
4:00		
5:00		
6:00		
7:00		
8:00		
9:00		
10:00		
11:00		
12:00pm		
1:00		
2:00		
3:00		
4:00		
5:00		
6:00		
7:00		
8:00		
9:00		
10:00		

Essential Daily Planner for Men

DATE

☐ ☐ ☐ ☐ ☐ ☐ ☐
Mon Tues Wed Thu Fri Sat Sun

	Appointment		**Office**

	General plan		**House**

	Reminder		

Time	Activity Description	Hobbies
12:00 am		
1:00		
2:00		
3:00		
4:00		
5:00		
6:00		
7:00		
8:00		
9:00		
10:00		
11:00		
12:00pm		
1:00		
2:00		
3:00		
4:00		
5:00		
6:00		
7:00		
8:00		
9:00		
10:00		

Essential Daily Planner for Men

DATE

☐ ☐ ☐ ☐ ☐ ☐ ☐
Mon Tues Wed Thu Fri Sat Sun

Appointment

Office

General plan

House

Reminder

Time	Activity Description	**Hobbies**
12:00 am		
1:00		
2:00		
3:00		
4:00		
5:00		
6:00		
7:00		
8:00		
9:00		
10:00		
11:00		
12:00pm		
1:00		
2:00		
3:00		
4:00		
5:00		
6:00		
7:00		
8:00		
9:00		
10:00		

Essential Daily Planner for Men

DATE

☐ ☐ ☐ ☐ ☐ ☐ ☐
Mon Tues Wed Thu Fri Sat Sun

Appointment

Office

General plan

House

Reminder

Time	Activity Description	Hobbies
12:00 am		
1:00		
2:00		
3:00		
4:00		
5:00		
6:00		
7:00		
8:00		
9:00		
10:00		
11:00		
12:00pm		
1:00		
2:00		
3:00		
4:00		
5:00		
6:00		
7:00		
8:00		
9:00		
10:00		

Essential Daily Planner for Men

DATE

☐ ☐ ☐ ☐ ☐ ☐ ☐
Mon Tues Wed Thu Fri Sat Sun

| | **Appointment** | | | **Office** |

| | **General plan** | | | **House** |

| | **Reminder** | | | |

Time	Activity Description	**Hobbies**
12:00 am		
1:00		
2:00		
3:00		
4:00		
5:00		
6:00		
7:00		
8:00		
9:00		
10:00		
11:00		
12:00pm		
1:00		
2:00		
3:00		
4:00		
5:00		
6:00		
7:00		
8:00		
9:00		
10:00		

Essential Daily Planner for Men

DATE

☐ ☐ ☐ ☐ ☐ ☐ ☐
Mon Tues Wed Thu Fri Sat Sun

Appointment		**Office**

General plan		**House**

Reminder		

Time	Activity Description	**Hobbies**
12:00 am		
1:00		
2:00		
3:00		
4:00		
5:00		
6:00		
7:00		
8:00		
9:00		
10:00		
11:00		
12:00pm		
1:00		
2:00		
3:00		
4:00		
5:00		
6:00		
7:00		
8:00		
9:00		
10:00		

Essential Daily Planner for Men

DATE

☐ ☐ ☐ ☐ ☐ ☐ ☐
Mon Tues Wed Thu Fri Sat Sun

Appointment

Office

General plan

House

Reminder

Time	Activity Description	**Hobbies**
12:00 am		
1:00		
2:00		
3:00		
4:00		
5:00		
6:00		
7:00		
8:00		
9:00		
10:00		
11:00		
12:00pm		
1:00		
2:00		
3:00		
4:00		
5:00		
6:00		
7:00		
8:00		
9:00		
10:00		

CPSIA information can be obtained
at www.ICGtesting.com
Printed in the USA
LVHW052148211222
735754LV00027B/494

9 781683 232544